To William
From
Julie Ann
xoxo

Other mini giftbooks in this series:
Notebook for a very special Daughter
Notebook for a very special Friend
Notebook for a very special Grandmother
Notebook for a very special Mother
Notebook for a very special Sister

Published simultaneously in 1996 by Exley Giftbooks in
the USA and Exley Publications Ltd in Great Britain.

12 11 10 9 8 7 6 5 4 3 2 1

Copyright © Helen Exley 1996.
ISBN 1-85015-789-8

Edited by Helen Exley.
Illustrated by Juliette Clarke.
Typeset by Delta, Watford.
Printed in Singapore.

Exley Publications Ltd, 16 Chalk Hill, Watford, Herts WD1 4BN, UK.
Exley Giftbooks, 232 Madison Avenue, Suite 1206, NY 10016, USA.

NOTEBOOK

For a very special
HUSBAND

Words selected and edited by
Helen Exley

Illustrated by Juliette Clarke

≡EXLEY
NEW YORK • WATFORD, UK

Bill - Happy 2nd Anniversary. I hope there are 142 more to come! Love, Julie Ann

Please keep this at work & when you feel stressed write to me; when you think of me, write to me. Give it back to me when it's full of your thoughts.

He is the one the flowers are always from.

TRISHA GOODWIN

He is the one that makes you feel like having
children - his children.
DIANE YOUNG

_____

_____

_____

_____

_____

_____

_____

_____

_____

_____

_____

_____

_____

A husband is a man who when someone tells him
he is hen-pecked, answers, yes, but I am pecked
by a good hen.
GILL KARLSEN

A husband is an expert at drying in between tiny toes
and fingers.
LYNN CUNNINGHAM

A husband is the only person whose socks you'd wash
without a shudder.
LINDA CORNISH

He is a man who stands by you through
all the troubles you wouldn't have had if you
had stayed single!

L.M. SMITH

A husband says "I love you" when you're wearing
a face-pack; and remembers your punch-lines
for you in public.

JILL WOODS

He's the guy who makes me say to God every day,
"Thanks for this guy, God".

VERONICA CASSIDY

_____

_____

_____

_____

_____

_____

_____

_____

_____

_____

_____

_____

When I pick the ricefield weeds
With the man I love,
The little weeds behind us
Are still there.
JAPANESE FOLK SONG

_____

_____

_____

_____

_____

_____

_____

_____

_____

_____

_____

_____

He lights my world with love and laughter.
He gives to all my days the warm promise of Spring, and
because of him I am ever young.

CATHERINE JENKINSON

_____

_____

_____

_____

_____

_____

_____

_____

_____

_____

_____

...For when I glance at you even an instant, I can no longer
utter a word: my tongue thickens to a lump, and beneath
my skin breaks out a subtle fire: my eyes are blind, my ears
filled with humming, and sweat
streams down my body....

SAPPHO (c. 612-580 B.C.)

A husband is the best friend you will ever have in your life. He will share your thoughts, your moods, your laughter and your tears. He is someone to live up to and to follow to the ends of the earth.

SUSAN HOLMES

_____

_____

_____

_____

_____

_____

_____

_____

_____

_____

_____

I know your eccentricities, your prejudices, your moods. And somehow, for some reason I can never fully understand, I am crazy with love for you.

CHARLOTTE GRAY, b.1937

_____

_____

_____

_____

_____

_____

_____

_____

_____

_____

_____

_____

_____

_____

In the arithmetic of love, one plus one equals
everything, and two minus one equals nothing.
NINON DE L'ENCLOS (1616-1706)

One of the oldest human needs is having someone
to wonder where you are when you don't come
home at night.

MARGARET MEAD (1901-1978)

Without you all streets would be one-way
the other way,...
Without you there'd be no one not to kiss
goodnight when we quarrel,...

ADRIAN HENRI

from *"Without You"*

_____

_____

_____

_____

_____

_____

_____

_____

_____

_____

_____

Lady Bird would crawl down Pennsylvania Avenue
on cracked glass for Lyndon Johnson.

JACQUELINE KENNEDY ONASSIS (1929-1995)

from "*The Tragedy of Lyndon Johnson*"

If ever two were one, then surely we.
If ever man were lov'd by wife, then thee.
ANNE BRADSTREET (c. 1612-1672)

You are the strong arms that protect me
through the night.

HELEN THOMSON, b.1943

When two people are at one in their inmost hearts, They shatter even the strength of iron or of bronze. Their words are sweet and strong....

I-CHING

Familiar acts are beautiful through love.

PERCY BYSSHE SHELLEY (1792-1817)

from *"Prometheus Unbound"*

A happy marriage is the best thing life has to offer.
It is built up brick by brick over the years
and cemented as much by the moments
of tenderness as by those of irritation.
JILLY COOPER

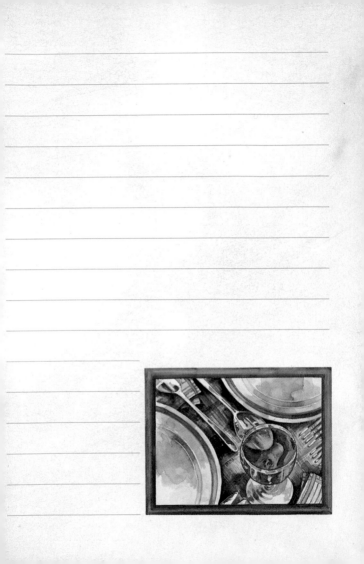

A successful marriage is not a gift;
it is an achievement.

ANN LANDERS, b.1918

_____

_____

_____

_____

_____

_____

_____

_____

_____

_____

_____

_____

I am in your clay.
You are in my clay.

KUAN TAO-SHENG (13th century A.D.)

Even after fifteen years it's like eating soup
with a fork, I just can't get enough of him.
JOANNE JONES

To be allowed to grow old together,
to continue to need and to feed one another,
"and the years forgot", must be every couple's hope.

HELGE RUBINSTEIN

_____

_____

_____

_____

_____

_____

_____

_____

_____

_____

_____

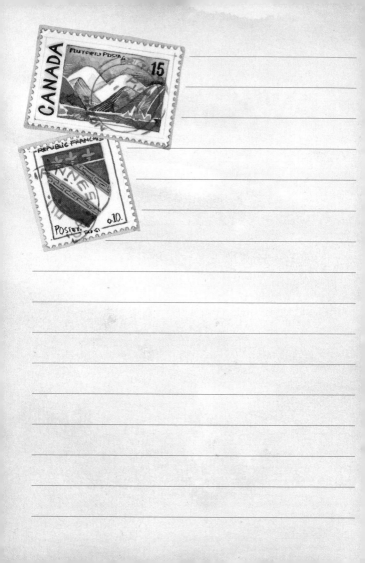

You are in my mind and in my heart. You are in the very
air I breathe. You are part of me.

ROSANNE AMBROSE-BROWN, b.1943

I love thee with the breath, smiles, tears,
of all my life!
ELIZABETH BARRETT BROWNING (1806-1861)